A Tim

The Development of Good Practice
in the Healing Ministry: A Handbook

CHURCH HOUSE
PUBLISHING

Church House Publishing
Church House
Great Smith Street
London SW1P 3NZ

ISBN: 978-0-7151-1070-6

Published 2000 for the House of Bishops of the General Synod of the Church of England by Church House Publishing.

This report has only the authority of the Working Party who produced it.

Cover inset image

On 23 January 1999, this image of a swirling disk of dust and gas surrounding a developing star called AB Aurigae was snapped by NASA's Hubble Space Telescope, showing unprecedented detail including clumps of dust and gas that may be the seeds of planet formation. Studying developing stars such as AB Aurigae, which is only 2 to 4 million years old and yet is 2.4 times more massive than our Sun, could provide an evolutionary missing link in the planet formation process. We are grateful to NASA and Carol Grady of the National Optical Astronomy Observatories for their help and for permission to use the image on the cover of this handbook and the main report.

Cover design by Beatrice Brandon.

Printed by Arkle Print, Northampton.

Contents

Membership of the Review Group

The Right Reverend John Perry

The Bishop of Chelmsford (Chairman)

Mrs Beatrice Brandon

General Synod member
and Researcher

Professor Gareth Jones

Professor of Theology, Christ Church
University College, Canterbury

Sister Hilary Markey CSMV

General Synod member,
Staff Member, Westminster Abbey
Healing Panel

Dr Althea Pearson

Chartered Counselling Psychologist
and Psychologist in Primary Care, NHS

The Reverend Canon Beaumont Stevenson

Psychotherapist, Chaplain
Oxfordshire Mental Health Care Trust
and Bishop of Oxford's Pastoral Care
Advisor

Assessors

The Reverend Malcolm Masterman

Training and Development Officer,
Hospital/Health Care Chaplaincy

Mr Jonathan Neil-Smith

Secretary, The House of Bishops,
Church House, London

The Right Reverend Dominic Walker OGS

The Bishop of Reading

The Reverend Canon John Gunstone

Former County Ecumenical Officer for
Greater Manchester and former Editor of
Healing and Wholeness

Dr David McDonald

Consultant Psychiatrist, Oxfordshire
Mental Health Care Trust and Home Office

The Reverend Canon Dr Paul Nener FRCS

General Synod member,
Chairman of Liverpool Diocesan Healing Panel
Sub-warden, Guild of St Raphael

The Reverend Michael Selman

Bishop of Exeter's Advisor on the Ministries
of Healing and Deliverance

Dr Gareth Tuckwell

Director, London and South East Areas,
Macmillan Cancer Relief and former
Director of Burrswood Christian Centre
for Health Care and Ministry

Secretary

Miss Jane Melrose

Church House, London

Foreword to the Main Report, *A Time to Heal*

The ministry of healing is one way in which the Church reaches out as part of its mission to the world, living out its commission from its gospel roots but in a way which is highly relevant to contemporary needs. There is a growing interest in the ministry of healing, with it playing an ever-increasing – and dynamic – role in the life of many parishes.

The House of Bishops is grateful to the Bishop of Chelmsford and his Working Party for this timely Report, which represents an important contribution to the Church's ministry in response to our Lord's injunction to heal the sick. I am happy to commend it for study and reflection, for action as appropriate in dioceses and parishes, and to all who are engaged in this vital part of the Church's pastoral ministry – often in partnership with others involved in healing and health care.

✠ George Cantuar

Preface

This handbook is published in conjunction with the much larger report, *A Time to Heal*, produced by a Working Party set up by the House of Bishops to review the ministry of healing. The handbook contains practical guidelines to encourage the development of the healing ministry in every parish throughout the country. It has been produced in an affordable form, using easily accessible language, to enable its wide circulation and use by clergy and laity, and to foster a common understanding of good practice.

In the extensive work of the Review Group on the major report *A Time to Heal*, we were greatly indebted to many other contributors. These include the large number of respondents to the comprehensive surveys. Among them, replies were received from other Provinces of the Anglican Communion and our ecumenical partners. The report has also drawn on the experience of bishops, clergy, hospital and prison chaplains, health care professionals and laity experienced in and committed to the support of the healing ministry.

A special tribute is due to Mrs Beatrice Brandon and Canon John Gunstone for their unflagging commitment in editing both the main report and this handbook.

The major report, *A Time to Heal*, and this associated handbook are offered as a contribution to and resource for the Church's ministry of pastoral care and evangelism in obedience to the commission of Jesus Christ to heal the sick. It is a gospel imperative!

✠ John Chelmsford

Chairman of the Review Group

1

Developing the Healing Ministry in the Parish

Introduction

In 1998, the House of Bishops commissioned a review of the ministry of healing, the first of its kind for over forty years, to assess both the theological understanding and the state of the ministry of healing in the Church of England. The terms of reference included making recommendations for its improved effectiveness, taking into account the activities of different groups within the Church of England and the ecumenical expression of this ministry. Over twelve months, a review group, including bishops, clergy, chaplains, health care professionals and other lay people, produced the report called *A Time to Heal*, which the House of Bishops agreed to publish for Pentecost 2000. This handbook presents some of the practical issues discussed in the main report, which should be consulted for more detailed study.

Healing, we might say, is what the Church's mission is all about. Healing, wholeness, salvation – these words embrace what God has achieved for us through the incarnation of Jesus Christ. His death, resurrection and ascension into heaven vindicated the truth of the gospel of the kingdom which our Lord taught. After his resurrection he commissioned his apostles to preach that gospel in the power of the Holy Spirit, so that men and women might turn to him and taste the first fruits of the kingdom in their own lives. In the power of the Holy Spirit, and in spite of her many failings, the Church has attempted to be God's obedient servant as a messenger of redemption, reconciliation, renewal – everything which the scriptures reveal to be in the purposes of God for his world and for the humanity he created and recreated in Christ.

The New Testament shows us that Jesus' healing of the sick and casting out demons were vivid demonstrations of the coming of the kingdom; and

1

his charge to continue that ministry in his name was part of his commission to the apostles. Through the ages the Church has responded by caring for the sick and troubled in many different ways – through pastoral care, prayer, the sacraments, spiritual gifts, deliverance ministries, practical friendship, and so on. But like all its work, the healing ministry is always in need of renewal as the Holy Spirit leads us to learn afresh what the New Testament teaches us about this ministry, as it has been handed down to us in our Christian tradition, and to recognize new opportunities for it in a changing society.

Before attempting to develop this ministry in a parish, questions need to be asked about why it has not been a visible part of normal everyday life so far, since the answers may give insights into the issues which need attention early on. Are there inhibiting factors such as disinterest and disbelief, misconceptions, misunderstandings, bad experiences and lack of confidence? We recommend that clergy and laity interested in developing the ministry of healing review how it is currently expressed in their parish.

The healing ministry in the parish is visionary . . . because it beckons us towards the future and a glimpse of the kingdom, the hope of creation renewed in perfect health and wholeness

The **healing ministry within the parish** needs to be founded on the theology of healing and to be expressed through preaching, teaching, and personal and corporate example. It gives us a glimpse of the kingdom – hope for the future, creation renewed and in perfect health. This ministry encourages each person in the parish to consider carefully and then look beyond their own circumstances and needs, to put their problems, challenges, weakness and suffering in perspective, and to seek healing and closer relationships through and with God, for themselves and for other people.

Sharing the vision with the congregation is an essential part of the preparations for establishing and developing a healing ministry. How its members respond to those seeking healing, comfort and support is part of the way in which the good news of God's love is spread. Every member of the congregation has a role in this ministry. By understanding its purpose and expression through prayer, each person can be helped to discern how they and their particular gifts from God may be most effectively used.

Furthermore, the support of the PCC for this ministry will affect, for example, the type of liturgy used, the style of service, the membership of the healing team, and the support and interest within the congregation. The issue to be addressed is 'What needs to be done to establish and develop the healing ministry as part of normal everyday life in *this* parish?'

The **ecumenical vision** of the healing ministry shared between the denominations and nurtured by God's grace is both prophetic and dynamic. A shared perception of its expression amongst our ecumenical partners shows how much we have in common and how our differences generally pale into insignificance compared to the opportunities to work together as one body in this ministry. The Holy Spirit is calling us towards a unity which is visibly expressed through words and action.

The **glimpse of the kingdom** revealed through this ministry gives us a vision of creation renewed. The parish church, its congregation and the local community must become aware of the healing needed within the whole of creation, particularly the local environment, how it suffers and how this affects those living within it. Misuse of God-given resources affects us all, not just in the present but in the future too. Recognition of where and how these issues arise locally is the first step towards the healing of the local environment.

The healing ministry in the parish is prophetic ... because it calls us to reconsider our relationships with God, each other and the world, and to seek forgiveness and a new start in our lives

So much unhappiness and ill health is connected to the state of our relationships with each other, our environment, ourselves and with God. We need to ask: What are the local issues? What kinds of reconciliation are needed? For example, the issues of greatest or most widespread concern may be broken relationships and families, unemployment, crime, social decay and vandalism, poverty, self-neglect, racism, and the effects of imprisonment on families and ex-offenders. Other key issues may be less visible, such as substance abuse, child abuse, domestic violence, AIDS, homophobia, infidelity, incest and occult involvement. The reasons individuals seek healing are diverse and sometimes inconspicuous; for example, bereavement, loss through separation and divorce, mental illness, physical illness, coming to terms with chronic or terminal illness, rejection because of sexual orientation, loneliness, anger and unresolved guilt. Illness may also be caused by social mismanagement, over-indulgence, oppression, fear and stress.

Such a wide range of concerns deserves more than one approach to healing. Jesus set us an example by using different approaches for different people, sometimes in public and sometimes in private. Sometimes they came to him for help and sometimes he went to them. The parish needs to consider the key local problems and how the Church can bring healing through ministry, pastoral care, mission and engagement with local challenges in prayerful and practical ways.

The concept of '**New Starts**' has shaped the preparations for the third Christian Millennium. Baptism and confirmation create a new start by incorporating an individual into the Body of Christ. Confession and absolution create a new start by restoring relationships within that Body (which is why it is more appropriately called 'the ministry of reconciliation'). Each of these gifts is from God. Through each the Church formally enables people to make a new start with God. They are expressions of the healing of the relationship between the individual and God. Unfortunately, many people, including some who attend church services, fail to appreciate fully these opportunities: they need encouragement and inspiring teaching in order to do so.

A new start with family and friends can be expressed through the sacrament of **marriage**, when two people are joined together for life in a new relationship with God. The 'Service of Prayer and Dedication after Civil Marriage' also helps to bring healing and a closer relationship with God through the recognition of public vows and commitment to each other, including 'in sickness and in health'. Services for the renewal of vows and thanksgiving for marriages at times of anniversaries are also opportunities for reconciliation and healing.

Many marriages sadly end in separation and divorce. How the parish church relates to divorced people will affect many people in the local community, including the children and grandparents. Each congregation needs to consider how to bring reconciliation and healing to broken families through the healing ministry, pastoral care, counselling, support groups, mission and fellowship. Some clergy have also found the study of a family tree to be a useful means of discovering broken relationships, traumatic events and family traits as well as disowned, lost, forgotten or unmourned relatives. People may also be helped by the 'healing of memories'. This term is used to describe a situation in which an individual is unhappily influenced by events which – though not necessarily consciously remembered – continue to affect their attitudes and behaviour. The Church through its ministry can help individuals to be freed from these burdens.

A new start for the **local community** may be found through addressing the key issues affecting local people. Racism and other forms of prejudice, for example, are painful and damaging. Memories may be very long and old resentments can burn away unresolved until a concerted effort is made by the local community to address the issues and seek reconciliation. The parish church has a role to play in bringing about the healing of deeply held memories which divide communities: the congregation at the heart of the community is called to bring people together and enable this to happen. As part of this dimension of healing within the community, the issue of how to welcome and reintegrate ex-prisoners and offenders is important. We have a duty to welcome people into our congregation, especially offenders, although this should be part of a carefully thought-out policy, in order to protect vulnerable people.

A new start for the **parish church** can be brought about through the healing ministry. The parish church is to be a sign and instrument of God's will, but because it is still imperfect, it is called to repentance, reform and renewal as part of its own healing. Realizing the visionary, prophetic and dynamic nature of the healing ministry provides a wonderful opportunity for the parish to review its priorities and mission.

A number of questions may arise during this process: How do the congregation, the PCC and the clergy relate to the key issues in the local community where healing is needed? How does this affect the services and liturgy used? What are the implications for reordering of the church building and the provision of facilities for disabled people? How does the healing ministry relate to existing ministry groups, lay training provision, parish mission statements, and financial budgeting for resources? How is it expressed through outreach, family care, pastoral care, lay visiting teams for the local hospital, links with local prisons, support for health-related mission overseas, care for the chronically ill and terminally ill, and their carers?

Through the ministry of healing in the parish, Jesus meets people at their point of need: not necessarily where the Church would like people to be, but where we truly are, in our brokenness and vulnerability. The healing ministry and its links with pastoral care within the parish need to be considered in the light of local needs and resources. Few parishes can do everything they would like to do or need to do. With prayerful reflection and practical appraisal, however, the local priorities can be agreed.

The **ecumenical expression** of this ministry is part of the healing process: the parish church can be a catalyst by finding prayerful, practical and visible ways of sharing this ministry. Clergy, ministers and laity within the denominations need to meet locally to discuss and plan the most appropriate ecumenical approaches. Issues to be considered in relation to joint healing services include the sharing of training, resources, information and support networks, and ecumenical hospital lay visiting teams. Wherever appropriate, opportunities to work ecumenically should be created and taken up, particularly in relation to healing, health care and related areas of pastoral care.

God's plan involves healing creation through Christ, the reconciler of all things: he is Lord and Servant who lives for the sake of the whole of creation. Issues such as animal welfare, reducing pollution and protecting wildlife, are part of our being reconciled to the rest of creation. The parish is the local environment and the parish church has a role in encouraging awareness of environmental issues and good use of resources. Furthermore, caring for and healing the local environment as part of God's creation is a task for the parish which often attracts the keen interest of young people.

Within the wider context, the healing ministry is also expressed through the support (including financial support) of overseas mission and charitable projects such as debt cancellation, health care provision, evangelism and education.

The healing ministry in the parish is dynamic . . . because Jesus is with us to the end of time: when we pray for his help, he comforts, strengthens and heals us, responding to our deepest needs

This ministry is an **integral part of our relationships** and **fellowship** within the Christian community and beyond. Jesus meets us at our point of need through each other.

Christ has no body now but yours, no hands but yours, no feet but yours. Yours are the eyes through which Christ's compassion must look out on this world. Yours are the feet with which He is to go about doing good. Yours are the hands with which He is to bless us now.

(Part of a prayer attributed to St Teresa of Avila)

God has gifted his Church in order to build up this ministry. Diocesan advisors on this ministry are a valuable resource for the congregation, and may be able to help through presentations, preaching, training and helping to set up local healing teams. They can also advise on the various ways in which this ministry is carried out and its wider implications, and help individuals to discern their vocation within it. Diocesan advisors also have useful contacts for information, resources, referrals, specialist advice, and ecumenical contacts.

The **laity** should be involved in this ministry if it is to be truly collaborative. Lay people may be interested in forming a healing team for services: care should be taken, however, to ensure that only suitable people are involved. Within the congregation there may already be people with relevant training and professional expertise, such as professional counsellors, psychiatrists and psychotherapists, whose gifts may be used through this ministry. Licensed lay workers such as pastoral assistants and youth officers may also be interested in involvement with the healing ministry.

Healing team members need proper **training** which should be ongoing and kept up to date. If clergy are not confident or prepared to train the team, or are untrained themselves, they should seek the help of the diocesan advisor. Those who are actively involved in this ministry also need the prayerful and practical support of the congregation, PCC and

7

clergy. Individuals who behave in an unacceptable way, however, should be withdrawn from the team; bad practice left unchecked brings the healing ministry and the parish church into disrepute and can lead to serious consequences for all concerned.

The **Eucharist** is the healing service *par excellence*. There the word of God is read and expounded; sins are confessed and forgiven; intercessions are made for the needs of the Church and the world, including the sick; the mighty acts of God in Christ are recalled and we partake of the sacrament of Christ's body and blood. The Peace exchanged during the Eucharist is a sign which impressively reminds us that what we are engaged in is a service for the healing of relationships through the grace of God.

The ministry of healing can be incorporated into the main Sunday service, offered through the laying on of hands either before or after receiving Holy Communion. Anointing is not usually regarded as a sacrament to be offered routinely as part of a Sunday service: it is sometimes offered after the service for those who need or request it. Whenever the laying on of hands or anointing are part of the service, the congregation needs to be properly instructed about what those who are ministered to should do and how those not directly involved should support the ministry with prayer.

Non-eucharistic services are ideal opportunities to involve members of the other denominations and the parish is encouraged to cooperate ecumenically in the planning and sharing of these services. Types of liturgies need to be studied, the theme of the sermon discussed, and the follow-up planned. A service of healing can be authentically Anglican without being exclusively so. Such a service can be a tangible expression of this healing of Christian divisions, showing a real willingness to work together and to share in each other's gifts and ministries.

Some people prefer to maintain a degree of anonymity; their attitude should be respected, even though it makes effective pastoral care more difficult or not possible. Others may feel unable to receive this ministry in a public setting because they are shy or afraid to show their emotions. So, as well as offering this ministry as part of services, there should be opportunities to receive it afterwards or in private. Care needs to be taken, however, when prayers for proxy healing are requested. Although sometimes people wish to receive the laying on of hands for others, opinions differ as to the appropriateness and use of this practice. This issue should be discussed with the PCC and the healing team members in order to form a locally acceptable view and to ensure that the privacy and dignity of those being prayed for is protected. There is a risk of confidentiality being breached if information about others is passed on in this context, particularly in a public service.

Christian Listening is a form of pastoral care related to the healing ministry, based on the ability, developed through training, to listen to others, to God, to the world and to ourselves. It provides the opportunity for individuals to be listened to and heard, and it can be appreciated as a precious gift, a sign that they matter, not just to the listener but also to God. This ministry of listening helps to bring about healing because it offers compassion and discernment. It is also, in a sense, the ears of the Body of Christ and can help in a broad way to inform the parish church of the needs of the local community (whilst ensuring that confidentiality is not breached).

Christian counselling and related ministries are valuable resources which should be carried out by people who are properly trained and under supervision. While all clergy are pastors, not all pastors are counsellors.

Pastoral care should not be confused with the work of professional counsellors and psychotherapists, who will have their own guidelines. Clergy and laity who are trained in counselling should make clear to parishioners what they consider appropriate and whether they are offering pastoral care or professional counselling. People who work in professional health care and related areas and who live in the parish can be valuable members of the healing ministry within the local church. They deserve to be treated with care and consideration since their work may make heavy demands on them and they should not be overburdened.

God also works through people beyond the Church, through **professional health care** and **social services**. The healing ministry should be carried out in a collaborative and cooperative manner, with health care professions and others involved in providing care whose particular contributions to the care of parishioners deserves to be recognized and respected. Wherever possible, links with the local health care and medical centres and surgeries should be encouraged. As complementary medicine and alternative therapies increasingly become available through local health care provision, the healing ministry also needs to be seen to be available and attractive. It is helpful to arrange from time to time local meetings of clergy and laity involved in professional health care in the local community, perhaps with a guest speaker, to encourage cross-disciplinary communication on health, healing and reconciliation issues.

Complementary medicine and **alternative therapies** are used by many people. In order to be objective about these approaches to health, it is necessary to be accurately informed about them. Those involved in the healing ministry and in related areas (particularly healing teams, pastoral care, counselling and listening, visiting and support networks) should be aware of the range of alternative approaches, including those which are linked with or involve the occult, and other factors which are incompatible with Christian teaching.

The parish may contain a **hospital** or **hospice,** in which case the hospital chaplain should be encouraged to be a member of the parish church and he or she will be a member of the local chapter. These local links can be valuable to both the parish healing team and to the chaplain. Through local networks, for example, hospital visiting teams may be formed. When parishioners are admitted to hospital it is courteous to inform the chaplain; this also helps to ensure that the spiritual needs of parishioners are cared for properly while they are in-patients. Links between the chaplains and the parish clergy also help to ensure the continuation of the healing ministry and pastoral care when parishioners are able to return home.

Prison chaplains appreciate links between local prisons and the parishes. Healing in the lives of prisoners depends to a large extent on being accepted after their release into society. The parish church can help by developing closer links with local prison chaplaincies, which are ecumenical, in order to be better prepared to accept ex-prisoners. There needs to be, however, a careful balance between involving the parish and protecting vulnerable people within it.

Prayer support is essential for everyone involved in the healing ministry – in the parish, the hospital, hospice and prison chaplaincies, in health care provision and pastoral care. Every person in the congregation is part of this prayer ministry, through private and corporate intercession, in personal prayer, prayer groups and in services. This is a valuable way of reassuring people who do not feel that they have 'special gifts' that they are a precious and valuable part of Jesus Christ's healing ministry.

It is helpful to have a wide awareness of the prayer ministry in the parish, so that when people are sick, those who love them and are concerned know whom to contact and can keep those praying up to date about their condition, within the boundaries of confidentiality. Some parishes for example, have a phone network through which news of patients can be spread for prayers. At the same time, many people are concerned about confidentiality and care needs to be taken to ensure that details are not made public or shared without the person's consent.

The formation and use of **networks** enable the effective exchange of information, sharing of resources, fellowship and support, and for developing a common understanding. It is helpful to have a list of contacts, including professional health care experts, psychiatrists and psychotherapists, diocesan advisors, charitable organizations specializing in this ministry, details of diocesan staff, including senior clergy for advice on pastoral issues, legal advisors, communication and youth officers, and relevant contacts in the other denominations and in the local area.

Training is a key concern in relation to this ministry. Clergy should take up opportunities for training which are available through Continuing Ministerial Education (CME), training programmes for clergy and laity by diocesan advisors and the recognized charitable trusts, as long as they are in line with the House of Bishops' draft guidelines for good practice. Clergy would also benefit from attending conferences and meetings with others involved in this ministry. Ordinands, particularly those on Ordained Local Ministry (OLM) training schemes, currently depend heavily on their parish placements to gain practical experience of this ministry. Such parishes should do all they can to ensure that ordinands are involved in it, and provide them with opportunities to learn and appreciate its diversity of expression.

When lay training programmes are being developed in the parishes, it is helpful to invite the diocesan advisors and to include people from the other main denominations in the planning of programmes and modules and related teaching, and to provide opportunities for learning from each other. Training should also include a wider appreciation of this ministry as it is carried out by the different traditions. In this way, the local expression of the healing ministry can be ecumenical and attractive to the widest range of people possible.

The **right environment** is important for the healing ministry. The Disability Discrimination Act 1995 stated that disabled people should have access to all buildings, including churches and church halls. A church that makes serious practical efforts to welcome disabled people gives them a sense of being wanted. Thought should be given to the environment in order to make healing services and other expressions of this ministry a safe and pleasant experience. A clean, well-lit, suitably heated and ventilated location, with comfortable seating, and easy access and facilities for disabled people and children are basic requirements, which also include a welcoming, peaceful and reverent atmosphere.

Effective communication is also important. Hearing loops, for example, are not a luxury but a basic need for those who have hearing or learning difficulties. They need to be used properly with an adequate sound system. Service sheets in large print are helpful to those who are partially sighted. The congregation, particularly those who are newcomers, need to have some idea of how they will be ministered to, in order to trust and to feel at ease. People involved in this ministry should be prepared to provide information for those with learning disabilities, language problems or mental health problems.

Pastoral care for those who receive the healing and deliverance ministries is particularly important. Although some people seek anonymity, many find that they benefit from receiving the healing ministry over a period of time, as healing is brought about at different levels and previously unacknowledged needs for healing may emerge. People's privacy and dignity should be respected. Care must be taken over confidentiality, the safe keeping of records, the issues of consent, and general safety, for those ministering and those receiving, whether in the church or elsewhere.

When setting up healing teams and introducing this ministry into services, provision should be made for the pastoral care needs which will follow. It is helpful to have vergers and sidespersons, who are sympathetic to this ministry and who have been trained or briefed to deal with enquiries and requests for help.

The care of people who are housebound is often left to members of the immediate family, creating a situation where individuals may be forced to give up their job or career and lose friends and hobbies, working for long hours without relief or respite. The ministry of healing can help carers within the parish to find a sense of peace and spiritual support which is much needed to cope with the day-to-day demands on their time, energy and emotions, and the strains which have been placed on their lives.

The **different stages in people's lives** and the **ways in which their need for healing may change** are part of the challenge facing those involved in this ministry. As people grow older, they eventually have to come to terms with their own mortality. Few people in our society are really ready to face death without fear and even fewer regard death as the ultimate healing opportunity. Within the parish, the implications for the local community and the impact of our ageing society should be discussed in relation to this ministry.

The healing ministry is also for **young people and children**. The pressures of examination times, trying to cope with the breakdown of family life (due to divorce or a member of the family having a custodial sentence), bullying, sexual abuse and peer pressure, for example, are areas where young people may seek help through the Church. Unfortunately, this ministry is not often explained to them and they may be quite unaware of it. Almost every parish includes young people and children; the healing ministry needs to be expressed in ways which they can appreciate.

Many young people are involved with drugs and other forms of substance abuse, which in turn affect their families, friends, studies and working lives, physical and mental health, spirituality and world-view. Young people also come into contact with the occult, through friends, the media's interest in this area, youth culture including computer games and heavy metal music. Some may only dabble on the fringe; others go on to become more involved and in increasing danger. The parish church is one of the few organizations which can help them, through the healing ministry. We strongly advise however, that the deliverance ministry should only be carried out in accordance with the House of Bishops' guidelines (1975) and that this is not an area of ministry for the untrained and unauthorized to 'have a go'.

Occasionally those involved in the healing ministry may become aware of claims or proven cases of **abuse**. They are recommended to follow the guidance for dealing with complaints set out in Chapter 2 on 'Good Practice'. It is also important that clergy and laity involved in this ministry are aware of current laws and Church guidelines relating to the protection of children and adults with learning disabilities, and the importance of confidentiality.

13

Regular reviews of the way in which this ministry is exercised within the parish, including all those involved, are a valuable way of highlighting the issues to be addressed before they become problems. For example, without a review, support for a particular type of service may wane while the need for a different approach may be ignored. The parish church needs to learn from experience in this ministry as with everything else it does. Being a pilgrim church involved in a dynamic ministry means being prepared to adapt and move on, not staying in the same place and being left behind.

One challenge sometimes overlooked by clergy and laity is the **willingness to be healed themselves** when necessary. We may be much encouraged ourselves when we are channels or instruments of others' healing; our loving empathy with others and our desire to help them through Jesus is a blessing to us. Nevertheless, it is important that we do not become so concerned about the healing and health of others that we neglect our own health and needs for healing. All of us need the healing ministry for one reason or another.

Developing the healing team

These suggested criteria assume that the PCC and congregation support the healing ministry within their parish and that the parish priest has a sound understanding of and some experience in this ministry. The criteria may need to be modified according to the nature of particular congregations, or when they are used to recruit members for deanery healing teams, but the basic requirements need to be kept in view.

Prayer and discernment

The basis on which a prayer ministry team exercises this ministry is that it is a group of Christians who pray together with faith, hope and love, seeking God's will.

❖ Individuals who feel called to be involved in healing teams should be willing to pray and listen, in order to discern where God is leading them in this aspect of the Church's mission and ministry; they need to be willing to grow in spiritual maturity.

❖ People involved in the healing ministry should be sufficiently self-aware to recognize their own spiritual, mental, emotional and physical needs for healing. A prayer life which acknowledges and is open to the healing love of Jesus Christ is essential, as is a willingness to recognize and seek healing for oneself, in order to be available as a channel of his grace. Sometimes people who feel drawn to be involved in a healing team are initially more concerned about seeking healing for themselves, which is why prayerful and patient discernment is such a valuable process before becoming part of a healing team. Nevertheless, the Church has always valued the role of the 'wounded healer' and individuals who have experienced some healing themselves can often be sensitive and valuable members of the team.

❖ Those seeking to be involved in this ministry need the support of others, through prayer and Christian fellowship, and willingness to support prayerfully the other team members. They also need to be willing to seek to love and serve them in Christ's name.

Personal qualities needed

❖ patience, with themselves, other team members and those seeking healing; maturity and self-awareness to help absorb the disappointments and hurts which can sometimes result through endeavouring to help others;

❖ humility; acknowledgement that healing comes from Jesus Christ, not the individual;

❖ acceptance of one's personal limitations, and willingness to refer those in need for specialist help, when necessary;

❖ compassion and empathy, in order to help discern the needs of others and the most appropriate and helpful way of ministering to them;

❖ the ability to listen, or learn how to listen, for listening is a great part of this ministry – listening to God and to other members of the team as well as to the one who is seeking help;

❖ reliability and trustworthiness; a willingness to work collaboratively in order to fulfil God's will.

❖ individuals seeking to join the healing team need to be well-known and regularly practising members of the parish church, enjoying the trust and confidence of the clergy and PCC.

In order to develop a common understanding of good practice, everyone involved in this ministry should be aware of and abide by the House of Bishops' draft guidelines for good practice in the healing ministry (see Appendix 1). People interested in joining healing teams should be provided with an opportunity to familiarize themselves with the guidelines and express their willingness to work within them, before being accepted into a team. It is essential that those who wish to be involved in healing teams understand the issues surrounding confidentiality (particularly in the local context) and accept the need for great care in the exchange and dissemination of information relating to those receiving this ministry and their close contacts. Individuals need to be realistic and fair about possible conflicts of interests and the potential difficulties of relationships in more than one capacity with other people in the local community.

A willingness to be accountable to and work under the leadership of the parish priest or chaplain is a key issue, as is the willingness to be appraised from time to time and, if necessary, be prepared to stand down from the healing team if circumstances indicate that this is advisable. Acceptance of the limitations of the kind of ministry which can be exercised by the healing team is also necessary.

Whilst mental and physical illness in general terms should not preclude people from consideration for membership of healing teams, a realistic and adequately informed assessment of an individual's physical and mental health and personal circumstances should be carried out, to ensure that those to whom he or she might minister would not be placed at risk in any way. Similarly, the personal behaviour of individuals should be such that they encourage public confidence in this ministry and do not put people off through inappropriate behaviour, or lack of self-awareness and personal care.

Individuals who are interested in joining healing teams should be able and willing to undergo training as advised by the parish priest, including training to keep up to date with developments in this ministry. They should also be committed to reading widely about this ministry and related areas.

Specialist skills and professional qualifications are not necessary but may be useful. However, those with specialist knowledge, particularly in health care, still need to work within the team under the guidance of the priest and according to the guidelines for good practice, when ministering as part of the healing team.

Cautions

'Wanting to be a "healer"': involvement of people who think they have special powers or 'have tingling hands' will need careful discernment. The source of healing in the Church's ministry of healing comes from Jesus Christ and this should be faithfully acknowledged by everyone involved.

Individuals who tell their priest that they are convinced that they have a gift of healing, and that God is calling them to exercise that gift more widely, need to be treated circumspectly, especially if they have recently transferred from another church. Difficulties can occur unless they are willing to submit to the pastoral leadership of a congregation.

'Spiritual bullying': whilst the healing ministry is a central part of the Church's mission, it is particularly relevant to the vulnerable and frail who need to be protected from over-enthusiasm, insensitive evangelism, inappropriate ministry or potential abuse.

Because the healing ministry is for everyone, including children and those with learning difficulties, care should be taken not to involve people who have a criminal record of abusing, exploiting or harming others.

We hope that by providing these suggested selection criteria for healing team membership, clergy and laity will be encouraged to work collaboratively to ensure that the healing ministry is a visible expression of the Church's mission in everyday life in the parish.

2

Good Practice in the Healing Ministry

Introduction

The healing ministry within the Church of England is increasingly becoming part of normal everyday life, expressed in many ways: publicly and privately, ecumenically and in cooperation with the caring professions. These detailed guidelines have been produced in response to requests from people and organizations involved in the ministries of healing and deliverance, taking into account their concerns. To some extent, they reflect the guidelines and codes of conduct and ethics already established for the medical and caring professions, and material produced by certain dioceses and healing organizations.

This ministry of healing is carried out within our society which reflects continually changing values and attitudes to health and healing. The Church of England's response is to seek to ensure that the ways in which it is carried out are theologically sound, responsible, loving and leading people to a closer relationship with God. The way in which we minister to people in need is one of the most important ways in which we spread the message of the gospel.

Key terms used in these guidelines are defined as:

❖   **health** – a dynamic state of well-being of the individual and society, of physical, mental, spiritual, economic, political and social well-being – of being in harmony with each other, with the material environment and with God (the World Council of Churches' definition in the report of its Christian Medical Commission);

❖   **healing** – progress towards health and wholeness;

❖ **disease** – a failure in ease, whether physical, mental or spiritual in location of pathology or disorder ;

❖ **deliverance** – release from evil spiritual influences which oppress a person or hinder the individual's response to God's saving grace;

❖ **clergy** – all persons ordained by the bishop as priest or deacon for service in the Church of England;

❖ **licensed lay ministers** – all lay persons licensed by the bishop to a ministry, for example, readers;

❖ **lay members of a healing team** – persons who have the approval of the local church congregation and parish priest to be involved in the healing ministry;

❖ **parishioners** – the persons to whom the clergy have a responsibility in the Church or community; parishioners may not necessarily be resident in the parish within which they receive the healing ministry.

The purpose of the guidelines

We need recognizable and acceptable standards of conduct for all those involved in the Church of England's healing ministry. A common understanding of what constitutes good practice will encourage everyone involved to maintain these standards. Guidelines for good practice are also a means of encouraging and retaining the confidence of parishioners and those ministering to them, affirming good practice where it already exists.

These detailed guidelines are a broad framework, relevant to everyone involved in the healing ministry, including those involved in the deliverance ministry, where additional care and safeguards are necessary. They are not intended to be overprescriptive, but to meet concerns about boundaries, provide good models of practice and point out key issues which need leadership and oversight. No framework, however, can cover every possibility or prescribe action and non-action for every situation which may arise. Clergy, licensed lay ministers and team members must determine which parts apply to particular settings and use them sensitively. It is recommended that everyone involved in the ministries of healing and deliverance should be fully aware of these guidelines.

The context

The healing ministry is part of the broad mission of the Church, expressed in the following ways:

❖ **publicly** as part of services:

- at healing services, including the Eucharist, baptism and confirmation;

- in institutions such as hospitals, hospices, nursing homes, residential homes for elderly and disabled people, prisons;

- at healing centres and related conferences;

- at Christian holiday venues, such as Spring Harvest and New Wine, which are often ecumenical.

❖ **privately** within the home, hospitals and hospices, discreetly in church side chapels, etc.

❖ **ecumenically** across the denominations, including local services, the hospital and prison chaplaincies

❖ **in cooperation** with the medical and caring professions.

The most common forms of healing ministry take place in the settings described above.

Public and private prayers of intercession

Christian worship has always included prayers of intercession customarily addressed to the Father through the Son and in the power of the Holy Spirit. Intercessory prayer, in which we pray individually and corporately for those who are suffering, combines our love with God's love and our will with his will, so as to cooperate with him in building his kingdom.

The laying on of hands

This action whereby a person or people lay hands on the head of someone has its origins in the Old and New Testaments and is associated with blessing, commissioning and healing. It takes place at confirmation and ordination and is included in modern liturgies for the ministry to the sick. Actions can often 'speak louder than words' and touch conveys a message of love and assurance as well as being a link with Christ's apostolic command to heal the sick. This form of touch can make those who are ill feel less fearful or alone in their suffering. Hands are usually placed gently on or side by side of the head, or on the shoulders, and accompanying prayers said quietly and reverently. The laying on of hands often takes place in silence (or when there are prayers, followed by silence).

Anointing

Anointing affirms our relationship with Christ who is 'the anointed one', and like water, bread and wine, oil is a natural resource which is blessed and used sacramentally in the ministry of the Church. We pray that as we are outwardly anointed with oil, we shall be inwardly anointed with the Holy Spirit. A sick person should be prepared for anointing and told what will take place. It is customary to anoint a person with thumb or forefinger, making the sign of the cross, with a small amount of oil on the forehead and sometimes the palms of the hands. Anointing is often accompanied by the laying on of hands and sometimes Holy Communion and reconciliation.

Reconciliation and absolution

Confession is increasingly seen as an act of reconciliation which begins with God calling us back to himself. The Anglican tradition values the use of a general confession as a communal act in the liturgy and makes provision for private confession to a priest. Private confession may be made in a formal or less formal setting and may include spiritual advice and counsel as well as absolution. Pronouncing God's love and forgiveness is a gift from God to the Church and its place in the 1662 *Book of Common Prayer* service of the 'Visitation of the Sick' indicates its significance in the ministry of healing.

Healing the family tree

The exploration of a family tree can enable some people to have a sense of belonging. The study of family trees can also be a useful means of discovering a possible explanation of broken relationships, lost or unmourned relatives, traumatic events and family traits. Pastoral counselling centred around a family tree may later be focused in a service of Holy Communion where members of an earthly family are remembered and brought into the healing love which is found in the Holy Trinity.

Healing of memories

Healing of memories is a term used to describe a situation in which individuals are unhappily influenced by things which – though not necessarily consciously remembered – continue to affect their attitudes and behaviour. In the healing of memories, the memory is not wiped out but its effect is no longer painful and debilitating. Professional counselling, prayer, the laying on of hands, anointing, confession and Holy Communion are among the appropriate means of bringing about the healing of memories.

Ministry to the sick

The Church has a distinctive role to play in the ministry to the sick because it has always linked the proclamation of the good news with healing. Modern health care and healing recognize the need to minister to the spiritual and religious needs of patients, as well as their physical needs. Christian ministry has a distinctive quality of love as well as a distinctive gospel message. This ministry of healing is therefore offered in love by the Church, explicitly by prayer, religious rites and chaplaincy, and implicitly by Christians engaged in many areas of ministry to the sick, such as doctors, nurses, carers and visitors. Christians minister to the sick in the name of Jesus and also to Jesus himself (Matthew 25.31f.).

Ministry to the dying

For Christians, death is not the end but a beginning, and the process of dying is often filled both with sadness and with hope for a fuller life with God. Hospice care in Britain has been pioneered by Christians, and modern medicine with its advances in pain control can enable people to die with dignity, and to prepare them and their loved ones for their death.

22

People facing death are often concerned about dying with broken relationships, unfinished business or a fear of what lies ahead. Here the Church can offer a ministry of reconciliation and the assurance that 'neither death nor life . . . nor anything else in all creation can separate us from the love of God, in Christ Jesus our Lord' (Romans 8.38,39).

Deliverance

It is a tradition for Christians to pray for deliverance from evil; the petition in the Lord's Prayer is an obvious example of this. Praying with people for their needs and protection is often an appropriate way of ministering to them. There are, however, some situations where a pastor is ministering to a disturbed person who appears or claims to be afflicted by a power of evil or an evil spirit. Inappropriate ministry may make matters much worse and the House of Bishops' guidelines should be observed (see the specific guidelines on pp. 32–3).

The wider implications

God's gifts of healing are occasionally experienced instantly or rapidly, but in most cases healing is a gradual process, taking time to bring deep restoration to health at more than one level. This ministry should not exist in isolation either; it relates in varying ways to other areas of Church activity including:

❖ pastoral care;

❖ spiritual development;

❖ the boundaries and overlap with the medical and caring professions, social services, etc;

❖ ecumenical cooperation, particularly at local level and through the chaplaincies;

❖ community issues, justice and equality issues and ethical matters, international issues;

❖ the whole mission of the Church, which could be described as healing in its broadest and deepest sense.

23

Directory of guidelines

The healing ministry is Jesus' ministry entrusted to us, always to be exercised with reverence, love and compassion. As a sound guideline, recognize the presence of God in those receiving this ministry and honour his presence in them.

It is important that the healing ministry is seen to be an example of best practice for others to look to and that it does not fall behind the best practice of secular institutions. Good practice is an issue for everyone involved in this ministry. *These guidelines are set out alphabetically for ease of reference and so that they can be understood and adopted as a whole framework.*

Accountability

Within the Anglican context, clergy and licensed lay ministers are accountable to their bishop. Lay team members should be accountable to their parish priest. Ultimately, all involved in the healing ministry are accountable to God for their actions and omissions. No one should work independently, believing that he or she is accountable only to God.

Clergy, licensed lay ministers, team leaders and members involved in this ministry need to be clear about the lines of accountability and who holds relevant authority within their church. Clergy in certain institutions have to work within a dual accountability to both their bishop and the institution which employs them.

Boundaries (see also Personal conduct)

It is important that all persons involved in the healing ministry know and acknowledge their limits of expertise and training and the limits of other team members; if limits are overreached, the risks increase. Everyone should be willing to seek advice and when necessary, to refer individuals to specialists, for example for professional counselling, medical expertise and the deliverance ministry. Good referral networks and their contact details should be developed and readily available. Any diocesan pastoral regulations relating to the ministries of healing and deliverance should also be observed by those ministering.

Clergy and lay healing team members need to develop an awareness of the personal boundaries which should be observed when dealing with troubled individuals. Hidden motives in the relationships between those ministering and parishioners need to be acknowledged sensitively.

Everyone involved in the healing ministry should develop an awareness of the psychological and emotional boundaries which must be respected. It is important to be to be able to identify and accept ownership when this situation is the result of personal needs or when it arises from the needs or projections of the person being ministered to. There is most risk when the situation is a powerful combination of the needs of both parties.

Child protection

Children are vulnerable: they must always be respected and ministered to with care. For clarification of responsibilities see the House of Bishops' Policy on Child Protection (1999). Awareness of legal constraints and of their full implications is essential. Follow the specific guidelines laid down in the Children Act 1989 for all activities on Church premises and when ministering to children elsewhere.

Christian Listening

Healing services rarely provide an ideal setting for listening in detail to an individual's situation and needs, so it is important to have appropriate facilities and structures outside the context of healing services and as part of pastoral care offered within the local church. Training in Christian Listening is strongly recommended for those who are interested in this form of ministry.

Collaboration

The healing ministry should be carried out in a collaborative and cooperative manner with health care professions and others involved in providing care; their particular contributions to the care of parishioners deserve to be recognized and respected. Clergy and lay team members need to be aware that other people involved in providing care are bound by codes of ethics and good practice. The concepts of good practice in these areas tend to have an educative effect on the public and can influence parishioners' expectations of accountability and good practice on the part of ministers.

Consideration should be shown when requesting help from professionals involved in health care provision who live in the parish. They may already feel pressurized by the emotionally demanding nature of their day-to-day work, without the added complications and stresses of a church-referred clinical burden. It is also possible that parishioners may be unaware of the professional codes by which professionals are bound and may have unreasonable expectations. If health care professionals are willing to be involved in the healing ministry in the parish, set clear guidelines and boundaries to ensure that they are not overburdened.

Collusion

Collusion should be avoided with people who attempt either deliberately or unconsciously to manipulate those who minister to them, either in counselling or prayer, with any diagnosis that is believed to be false, especially in relation to the deliverance ministry.

Competence

All persons involved in the healing ministry need to ensure, and continue to monitor, that they (and other members of the healing team) are properly prepared and fit to be involved in this ministry. This involves being willing to consider seriously any concerns expressed about the competence of any member, including oneself. If one's personal fitness or that of another team member is in doubt or compromised, it is important to recognize when the individual affected should withdraw because of, for example, personal or emotional difficulties, illness, substance abuse, exhaustion or conflicts of interest.

Complaints

The complaints procedure is in itself straightforward, provided that it is clear against whom a complaint is being made. Complaints about a member of the clergy (ordained person – this does not cover readers or lay pastoral workers) are currently covered by the complaints procedure in the Ecclesiastical Jurisdiction Measure 1963. Complaints about clergy should be made to the bishop who has disciplinary power over them. Complaints about a lay person are not covered by Church of England legislation, so only if the complaint verges on areas of criminal activity would the Church ask the police to investigate.

The substance of what complaints can be made about and the standards against which complaints can be compared are difficult areas because of lack of written or authoritative norms against which appropriate behaviour can be assessed. Where guidelines for good practice are established, these may reasonably be used as a benchmark against which behaviour and related complaints could be measured. Recognition and implementation of the House of Bishops' guidelines for good practice in the healing ministry and the guidance in this handbook, provide a framework for objective assessment of complaints and help to discourage the kind of behaviour from which they could arise.

If members of a local healing team are operating under the control of the clergy and have been trained or prepared by them for this ministry, then a complaint could be made to or against the clergy if team members behave in an abusive or unacceptable way. If, however, laity become too exuberant or over-intense and/or carry out the healing ministry independently, it would be unreasonable to discipline clergy for a situation beyond their control.

Certain types of behaviour are liable to result in complaints. Within the ministries of healing and deliverance, there is scope for unwitting or even deliberate abuse, and ministers who are self-aware will know of the temptations and dangers which can arise. For example, certain forms of humour, innuendo, flirting and touch can be interpreted as sexual harassment.

More serious forms of abusive physical contact can amount to a criminal offence. The victim may feel unable to complain because of fears of not being believed or even be misled into thinking that the abuse may bring some benefit, spiritually or psychologically. Complaints of such behaviour should be taken seriously and treated sympathetically and sensitively.

Anyone who suspects misconduct by another person involved in the ministries of healing and deliverance, which cannot be resolved or remedied after discussion with the person concerned, should implement the complaints procedure, doing so without breaches of confidentiality other than those necessary for investigating the complaint.

Allegations of sexual abuse, including that of children, may be made or become known. The House of Bishops' Policy on Child Protection (1999) provides guidelines for cases of alleged abuse of children. Furthermore, each social service department has a local code of practice for child protection and investigation. In the case of adults with learning disability, sexual abuse of them is a criminal offence. Allegations by other adults of abuse may be appropriately investigated by the police and lawyers.

The insurer should be given immediate notice of any incident that might lead to a claim. Failure to comply with this requirement may prejudice any cover provided. Clergy should also be aware of the provisions of Canon Law as set out in Canon B 29 of the Ministry of Absolution and the Proviso to Canon 113 of the Code of 1603.

In the first instance, complaints about a lay healing team member should be referred to the priest in charge of the healing ministry team. If the complainant is not satisfied with the outcome of this referral, the complaint should be referred on to the archdeacon. Where lay healing team members are found to have behaved in an unacceptable way, they should be removed from the team and not involved further in this ministry.

Confidentiality

People's privacy and dignity should be respected and protected; most people do not want to discuss their problems publicly or to be overheard by strangers. Parishioners are entitled to expect that the information they give in the context of the ministries of healing and deliverance will remain confidential and not be misused in any way. Everyone involved in these ministries should be sensitive to the issue of confidentiality, which is a means of providing people with safety and privacy. Betrayal of confidential material destroys trust. Those involved need to be told of any limitations to confidentiality which may arise.

Care must be taken not to pass on personally identifiable information through overlapping networks of confidential relationships. Confidential information should not be shared or made available to others, including members of the family, friends or partner, either of the parishioner or the person entrusted with confidential information, except where agreed upon with the parishioner.

The right of the parishioner to share personal information with one member of the healing ministry team and not with another should be safeguarded. On the other hand, team members should also be aware of the danger of being manipulated and divided by a parishioner sharing personal information with more than one member of the team.

Disclosure of confidential details in public and semi-public intercessory prayer, on prayer boards, in prayer lists, etc., should be avoided. Confidential details must not be used in the production of video and audiotape recordings for training or publications, reports or conferences, except with the express permission of everyone involved.

It is important not to promise confidentiality without some qualification; for example, if what is confided involves criminal activity, abuse of children or harm to others. Exceptional circumstances may arise which give good grounds for believing that serious harm may occur to a person being ministered to and/or other people involved. In such circumstances, after careful consideration and before disclosing any confidential information, the consent of the person concerned should be sought whenever possible unless there are also good grounds for believing that they are no longer willing or able to take responsibility for their own actions. In such cases, those ministering should, if possible, consult with someone in a position senior to themselves before taking action which may well take the case out of their hands. The parishioner involved should be informed that such disclosure has taken or will take place.

Any disclosure of confidential information should be restricted to relevant information, conveyed only to appropriate people and for appropriate reasons likely to alleviate the exceptional circumstances. The ethical considerations include achieving a balance between acting in the best interests of the parishioner and the minister's responsibilities to the wider community.

Conflicts of interest

No one involved in the healing ministry should use his or her position within the ministries of healing and deliverance to establish or continue any improper personal relationship, with the purpose of receiving any personal advantage or gain, whether monetary, emotional, sexual or material. Clergy and lay team members should beware of any gift, money, favour or hospitality which might be interpreted as seeking or exerting undue influence or leave opportunities for accusations of charging for the healing ministry.

It is important that those ministering are aware of the needs of the parishioner and act with compassion, whilst keeping a proper emotional and psychological distance. All persons involved in this ministry must be aware of their own emotional needs and of the possibility of exploiting vulnerable people to meet these needs.

Particular risks exist for the abuse of power and conflicts of interests in dual relationships, such as those between team members. At all times, the well-being of the parishioner is paramount and the boundaries of the relationship should be made clear, without rejecting the other person. If the boundaries are unacceptable, it may be advisable to end the pastoral relationship in the best interests of both parties.

Consent

It is important to ensure that every person knows and understands how he or she is going to be ministered to and that he or she consents, before receiving the healing or deliverance ministry. For this reason, it is necessary to include a brief but clear description of the ways in which the ministry will be carried out before or at the beginning of a service, for example, for the benefit of newcomers. Please note that there is only proof of consent if this is provided in writing by the parishioner, although in many instances this is not practical.

People of full age (18 years and over) and of ordinary mental capacity should be allowed to consent. The issue of consent should be revisited if the purpose or nature of the healing ministry approach alters; for example, the healing ministry leading to the deliverance ministry. People should be encouraged to ask questions whenever they are in doubt.

Consent should not be taken for granted. Individuals should not be ministered to against their will. The right of people to decline the healing and deliverance ministries must be respected. It is easy, for example, to assume that those sitting in wheelchairs in a healing service are there for the laying on of hands; those ministering should not just assume that they want prayer for their mobility.

Sensitivity is essential in relation to issues of power and control, particularly in institutional and high-dependency settings and those involving children and families. Care should be taken in those situations where a parishioner's ability to make informed choices may be impaired; for example, because of learning disabilities, serious illness, severe pain and emotional distress, or heavy medication.

It may be necessary for those involved in the ministries of healing and deliverance to make a judgement about the competence of persons over 18 years of age, to make an informed decision involving their consent. If someone is not capable of informed consent, consent should be obtained from the person who has the legal authority to give it on the parishioner's behalf. Even if the person with legal consent has given it, there may be circumstances when parishioners (children or adults) have expressed a strong view that they do not want to be ministered to, in which case their view should be respected.

The feelings and wishes of children being ministered to should be sensitively taken into consideration for example, children should not be ministered to against their will. Ensure that adequate safeguards are taken to prevent exploitation, neglect and physical, sexual or psychological abuse.

The consent of parishioners must be gained before sharing their confidential details with other parties such as professional workers, medical doctors or psychiatrists.

Cooperation

People need to find a closer, deeper relationship with God as far as is possible and to be active partners in their healing. Parishioners' needs should be discussed with them in order that the healing ministry can proceed with caution and with informed consent.

Counselling

Pastoral care, which has great value and is one of the ways in which we carry out the mission of the Church, should not be confused with the work of professional counsellors and psychotherapists who will have their own guidelines and indemnity. While all clergy are pastors, not all clergy are counsellors.

Clergy and laity who are trained in counselling should make clear to parishioners what they consider to be appropriate *and must make clear whether* they are offering pastoral care or professional counselling. Consideration needs to be given to the issue of how the relationship between the minister and the parishioner may be affected in other contexts. Professional counsellors should adhere to the codes of ethics and practice of their regulatory organizations and observe the need for professional insurance cover.

Debriefing (see also Confidentiality)

Team members or partners working together in the healing ministry need to meet regularly to debrief each other and, when appropriate, pray together. Care should be taken, however, not to breach confidentiality.

Deliverance

This is an area of ministry where particular caution needs to be exercised, especially when ministering to someone who is in a disturbed state. The House of Bishops' guidelines (1975) on the deliverance ministry should be followed and cases referred to the diocesan advisors when necessary. The advisors' special expertise should be used in order to help as effectively as possible those who think they need this ministry.

The House of Bishops' guidelines (1975) on the deliverance ministry state that the following factors should be borne in mind:

1   It should be done in collaboration with the resources of medicine.

2   It should be done in the context of prayer and sacrament.

3   It should be done with the minimum of publicity.

4   It should be done by experienced persons authorized by the diocesan bishop.

5   It should be followed up by continuing pastoral care.

Diagnosis and discernment

Superficial and hasty judgements are to be avoided: time should be taken, as far as is practical, to listen carefully and make a thorough assessment of the parishioner's needs, as part of an initial diagnosis to make an informed decision about the most appropriate form of healing ministry for them.

There is an important distinction between diagnosis and discernment. Diagnosis is done intellectually and involves clear distinctions between types of conditions. Discernment is a spiritual gift and is the prayerful choice between different courses of action where there are no clear signs or definitions of condition or need.

It usually takes time for the healing ministry to be effective at different levels in each individual. Further needs may emerge and it is important not to be overhasty. Through prayer, the ways in which God is healing the parishioner and how he or she can best be helped may be discerned.

Ecumenical and interfaith issues

Sensitivity and general awareness are necessary. The healing ministry is the point at which people mix most readily across the denominations and can be a time when they are very vulnerable. The healing ministry should be carried out in cooperation, where appropriate, with clergy and representatives of other denominations. The development of the ecumenical expression of the healing ministry needs to be encouraged, wherever possible.

Sometimes people of other faiths also attend healing services and may need particularly sensitive assistance, taking into account their world-view.

Emergencies

Even in extreme cases, it is rarely necessary to act immediately. It is very helpful primarily to establish an atmosphere of calm. Persons involved in the healing ministry should not allow themselves to be pushed into actions through other people's expectations and insistence. If something quite unexpected happens, it may be necessary to reconsider the approach and, if necessary, stop ministering.

Those ministering need to be attentive towards the person for whom they are praying. If someone becomes very distressed or noisy, assistance should be sought to help the individual to be taken to another place if possible and then to calm the situation down.

Ethical issues (see also **Accountability** and **Supervision**)

Clergy and laity may find themselves caught between conflicting ethical principles which could involve issues of public interest or private conscience. In these circumstances, it is advisable to consider the particular situation in detail and, if necessary, the issues should be discussed with the diocesan advisor and/or someone who is senior to the people involved. Even after conscientious and prayerful consideration of the ethical issues involved, some dilemmas cannot be resolved easily or wholly satisfactorily. Supervision can be helpful in providing a source of objective advice on ethical issues.

Expectations

There should be:

❖ an expectation and belief that God is, as ever, at work in society and in individuals, communities and the whole creation;

❖ an openness to the unexpected, unusual and even the embarrassing;

❖ and, equally, a thankfulness for the 'ordinary' everyday miracles and signs of God's healing touch, which are too easily taken for granted.

Gifts of the Spirit (see also Discernment)

Certain individuals, groups or communities are used by God in ministering powerfully in various areas of the healing ministry. These charisms are often related to natural gifts (for example, in the medical and nursing professions), but sometimes they are manifested without any connection with human abilities. Such gifts of the Spirit should be received with thanksgiving and yet with wisdom and discernment (see 1 Corinthians 12.1-11).

Those who exercise these gifts need to be helped to minister humbly, with the support of their congregation and under its leadership. Spiritual gifts can often become more effective if those who exercise them learn from others and accept further training, but in some cases a charism of healing may be manifested only once in a person's experience.

Hospital chaplains

The special ministry of hospital chaplains should be recognized and respected, and the usual courtesies observed when informing them of the admission of patients. Chaplains should be encouraged to be members of a local church for mutual support and benefit.

Influences

Everyone involved in the healing ministry needs to have a sound grasp of the theology on which it is based. This is the responsibility of everyone involved but particularly the clergy and other team leaders.

The healing ministry is non-judgemental: those involved in it are encouraged to consider and address their own prejudices and stereotyping to avoid projection of their personal internal codes of behaviour, which could lead to unreasonable expectations being placed upon other people. People involved in this ministry should not be easily shocked, should the emotions of those receiving ministry be released.

The introduction of concepts or imagery which are more commonly associated with New Age approaches to healing, such as crystals and pendulums, should be avoided.

Information (see also Confidentiality and Public statements)

Informed consent: people have a right to know what is being provided and to have some idea of how they will be ministered to, in order to trust and to feel at ease. Information must be in a readily accessible form which people, including the unchurched, can understand; for example, clear and jargon-free pew leaflets can be very helpful. People involved in the healing ministry should be prepared to provide information for those with learning disabilities, language problems or sensory impairment, and those with mental health problems.

A sensitive balance is needed between strengthening faith in God and avoiding statements which are likely to lead to misunderstandings and unrealistic expectations. Avoid overemphasis on physical expressions of healing. It is preferable to encourage a deeper understanding of healing of the whole person, through Christ. The healing ministry provides opportunities for further reflection and a deeper understanding of the Church's mission, which embodies healing in the broadest sense.

Insurance (see also Child protection)

Public liability insurance is usually provided as part of a package of cover for parishes. The following comments relate to cover provided by the Ecclesiastical Insurance Group (EIG) under their Parishguard policy; please refer to the wording of the policy cover for other Church organizations, or if cover is provided by another insurer. In simple terms, Parishguard covers healing ministry activities of the clergy and others authorized by the PCC (being anticipated as a normal function of ministry with the awareness of the rural dean or archdeacon). Indemnity is provided for legal liability arising from accidental bodily injury or damage to property. There are special cover extensions for 'administrative errors or omissions' and 'pastoral care'. An optional extension is available for professional counselling. Alternative arrangements for insurance cover for professional counsellors may also be available through an individual's professional regulatory body.

The Church of England has recognized the various complex issues surrounding the deliverance ministry. It has sought to centralize its expertise and maintain a measure of control via a specialized diocesan appointment. Extensions of insurance cover are available for a range of professional diocesan roles such as the authorized diocesan deliverance team. Deliverance ministry is not regarded by EIG as a general parish activity; an individual parish should consult its insurers on any liability risk which might reasonably be seen as a special activity or function.

All reasonable steps should be taken by those involved in the healing ministry to ensure awareness of current law as it applies to this ministry; for example, some approaches might be misconstrued as assault if carried out without clear ongoing consent. The insurance does not cover the perpetrator of a criminal act, such as abuse or assault, although a measure of insurance exists for legal expenses in certain situations. With an increasingly litigious society and expectations of higher professional standards, insurers regularly review the cover provided by their policies and must pursue a 'risk management' approach to prevent claims. It is imperative that those involved in the healing ministry operate within authorized codes, with appropriate supervision, and adhere to current best practice.

Introducing healing services

It is important to safeguard the proper representation of lay people in the decision-making processes related to healing services. The PCC and congregation need to understand and support the concept and those involved, before healing services are introduced. If a regular liturgical healing service is to be held in a parish church, the PCC should approve its use by resolution.

The cooperation of those in the congregation with medical and nursing training is highly desirable at an early stage. Where appropriate, local medical centres and surgeries should be informed of the ministry being offered in the parish church.

Language

The language used should be inclusive and sensitive to the situation, understandable and acceptable to those receiving the healing ministry. Excessive noise levels are not conducive to an atmosphere of peace, love and patient hope.

Networks for advice, support and referrals

The telephone numbers of relevant contacts should be available for emergencies. It is helpful to develop networks for advice, support, resources and referrals, including people in the caring professions and social services and other secular networks, if appropriate. The contact details for the diocesan advisor on the deliverance ministry should also be readily available for clergy and healing ministry team leaders, but not passed to those seeking help in this area, as a general rule.

Non-discrimination

The healing ministry is available for everyone. There is no place for discrimination of any kind. The common humanity and uniqueness of each individual must be respected and valued.

Non-exploitation

The healing ministry is non-exploitative. Clergy and team members must not exploit emotionally, sexually or financially those receiving the healing ministry. Emotions are sometimes released during this ministry which can leave the person feeling vulnerable. No one who receives the healing ministry should be put under emotional pressure or manipulated, particularly through guilt or fear. Furthermore, no pressure should be put on people to give premature testimony of healing.

Clergy in particular, because of their role as pastors, spiritual guides and representatives of the faith, need to be aware of the issue of power and their position of comparative strength. Authority explicitly derived from God is particularly awesome and yet can be misused, consciously or unconsciously. Those ministering are encouraged to seek in all humility and love to keep in touch with the vulnerability and weakness which the parishioner may be feeling.

Clergy and lay team members should also seek to recognize their own emotional needs and ensure that these are met outside involvement in the healing ministry. Care and sensitivity are needed to ensure that this ministry is not used to make parishioners dependent on those ministering to them.

Personal conduct

General manner and appearance: the way in which clergy and lay team members behave with courtesy and consideration is part of the message of the gospel. First impressions count. It is considerate to dress appropriately and be conscientious about personal hygiene. The distinction between informality and intimacy is important. Informality can put people at ease, intimacy can lead to overfamiliarity and unnecessary risks.

When two or more people meet, messages can be conveyed verbally and also non-verbally through body language; for example, stance, posture, repeated movements and facial expressions. All such methods of communication can be used to make the most of healing opportunities, or knowledge of their use can be abused and lead to domination, manipulation, exploitation or misunderstanding of motive, and lack of trust.

The ways in which people communicate non-verbally give out powerful signals, which may be different from those consciously intended. Touch should be used with care and forethought. Used in the right context, it can be an important element in conveying comfort and healing. Used carelessly, touch can be dangerously ambiguous.

Any form of sexual advance or contact between those ministering and the parishioner in the context of the ministries of healing and deliverance is unacceptable, harmful and grounds for allegations of misconduct.

Prayer

Since the healing ministry is based on prayer in the name of Jesus Christ, those ministering should be helped to grow in their personal spirituality. To minister sensitively to others, they should be guided in the use of both formal and spontaneous prayer.

Intercessory prayers are best when succinct and accompanied by periods of silence so as to focus on God. When praying for people by name in public, it is pastorally desirable to ask for their permission to do so. Some may not wish their illness to be known for personal, work or family reasons. Sensitivity also needs to be exercised in giving details of people's illnesses. Prayer may need to be informed but the purpose of intercession is to hold people before God and not to provide information, spread gossip, or give clinical diagnoses and reports of personal opinions of someone's condition..

Prayer support

Prayerful support for everyone involved in the healing ministry, caring professions and the wider Church, including hospital and prison chaplains, is important and to be encouraged. Those involved in the deliverance ministry particularly need daily prayer support from friends and colleagues and their local community.

Proof of healing

People should be encouraged to recognize God's healing power in everyday and ordinary events, improved relationships with others, and particularly in their deepening relationship with God, rather than depending exclusively on 'signs and wonders'. Phenomena that can accompany this ministry, for example being 'slain in the Spirit', can sometimes be a genuine expression of release and acceptance of God's healing touch, but they are not always a measure of true healing and should not be sought for their own sake.

Proper preparation

The daily prayer-life of clergy and lay team members is an essential factor in the way in which they can be used in the healing ministry, and its quality is reflected in the way in which they minister and relate to other people. Before carrying out this ministry, it is important to make time for prayer, personal and corporate, and if possible reflection, receiving Holy Communion and fasting in certain circumstances. Plans for any follow-up ministry which may be necessary and for the unexpected should be in place. All team members need to be properly aware of these plans in advance.

Proxy healing

The practice of intercessory prayer has always included the provision for worshippers to intercede for other people for whom they are concerned. Although sometimes people wish to receive laying on of hands for others, opinions differ as to the appropriateness and use of the practice of proxy healing. This issue is worth discussion within the PCC and healing teams, in order to form a local view on the acceptability of proxy healing.

It should be borne in mind that proxy healing should not in any way breach confidentiality or betray trust through intermediaries requesting prayers for others not present. Those ministering to individuals requesting proxy healing on behalf of others should be alert to the potential harm which could be done when confidential details are passed on as part of requests for prayer ministry, particularly in public and semi-public settings.

Public statements (see also Confidentiality, Information and Representation)

Good relations with the media are vital, for we rely on journalists to communicate Church affairs to the wider public through the press, radio and TV. Interest in the ministries of healing and deliverance in these circles is considerable, and there have been some interesting and inform-ative articles and programmes on these topics in the past. However, certain sections of the secular media can exploit those who make public statements about their healing: it is helpful to consider how to deal with these issues effectively before they arise. Many dioceses run courses on how to respond to the media.

All public statements and advertising should be accurate as far as possi-ble. No one should be pressurized into making public statements until they are ready and willing. It is important to avoid making false or exag-gerated claims or statements which cannot be adequately supported and which could exploit people's vulnerability or lack of knowledge. Nothing should be offered which cannot be guaranteed. No one should be led to believe they are being offered something, for example a guarantee of cure, which is in fact not being offered. Clergy and lay team members need to be aware of legal decisions involving the Advertising Standards Authority etc., and it is advisable to keep a record of conversations or interviews with the media.

Personal statements which may be construed as the official view of the Church should be avoided. Clergy and lay team members should be aware of, and use if necessary, the Church structures – diocesan communications officer, Archbishops' Council spokespersons, House of Bishops' appointed spokespersons and so on. Where information is recorded, it will almost inevitably be edited and therefore potentially subject to misrepresentation. It is advisable to insist on seeing the edited version prior to transmission, if at all possible.

Reconciliation

The Anglican attitude towards confession has sometimes been described as 'all may, none must, but some should'. The Church pronouncing God's love and forgiveness is a gift from God and its place in the service of the 1662 *Book of Common Prayer*'s service 'Visitation of the Sick' indicates its significance in the ministry of healing.

Canon B 29, concerned with the ministry of absolution, makes reference to the unrepealed proviso to Canon 113 of the Code of 1603 concerning what is commonly called the 'seal of the confessional', by which a priest hearing a confession is 'charged and admonished' not to reveal anything committed to his or her trust and secrecy under 'pain of irregularity'. It is widely and generally accepted therefore, that whatever is said to a priest by a penitent during a private confession is accorded total confidentiality. When in doubt, however, priests may go to their bishop or another priest with what happens in the confessional for supervision, maintaining of course the anonymity of the person making the confession.

Records (see also Confidentiality)

Where appropriate, and with the individual's permission, it is helpful to keep adequate records, including relevant details of appointments and meetings involving the ministries of healing and deliverance, always taking into account the need for confidentiality. Comparison of notes taken on different occasions may reveal issues not openly expressed which may help to find the most appropriate form of healing. Parishioners need to be assured of the utmost confidentiality. Records should include only such information concerning parishioners and others involved as is strictly necessary, and exclude superfluous information, particularly that which could be potentially embarrassing or damaging.

It is the responsibility of clergy and lay team members to be aware of any changes to legislation and regulations concerning rights of access to records. To ensure confidentiality, written and other portable forms of records must be kept in a secure place such as a locked filing cabinet. Stored information including computer-based records is subject to statutory regulations such as the Data Protection Act. All those who keep such records should be aware of the necessity to register under the Act.

The records kept need to contain accurate relevant information to assist those ministering and caring for the person, as it may be advisable, after gaining the parishioner's permission, to share notes/records with other professions (such as medical practitioners and psychiatrists in relation to the deliverance ministry).

Accusations and incidents of wrongful acts may only come to light after a long period of time, perhaps many years. Whilst it is difficult to be prescriptive, special thought should be given to safeguarding records on an indefinite basis, particularly if an individual case is complex in nature or involves children under 18 years of age. An analogy can be drawn with current employment practices which require the retention of records for a minimum period of 40 years. Case law continues to revise the boundaries of the Limitation Acts. Where records are clearly no longer needed arrangement should be made for their secure disposal.

Representation

Clergy and lay team members should always set an example of good practice and not behave or allow others involved to behave in ways which would undermine confidence in the Church or the ministries of healing and deliverance. Behaviour should be such as to embody the communication of the gospel and to uphold and enhance the good standing of the Church as a body concerned with the pastoral care and well-being of everyone.

Reviews

Regular reviews should be undertaken of the way in which the healing ministry is carried out locally, with those involved. For example, support for local healing services can vary and a regular review may highlight the issues to be addressed before they present serious problems.

Responsibility for 'follow-up'

Those carrying out the healing ministry need to make adequate provision for follow-up as part of normal pastoral care, for example, bereavement counselling, home visits for the housebound to receive this ministry, prayer support through healing prayer groups and intercessions in public services. In particular, continuing support and care for those who have received the deliverance ministry is an important factor in their healing and strengthening.

Safety (see also **Situations to avoid**)

All reasonable steps should be taken to promote and ensure the safety of everyone involved, including team members, the congregation and particularly those receiving the healing ministry. When individuals find themselves in situations which make them uneasy, they should try to identify whether the fears are rooted in reality and take sensible and calm action to avoid placing anyone at risk.

When individuals who are standing receive the laying on of hands, there is the possibility that the person will fall to the floor. In some circles this phenomenon is described as 'being slain' or 'resting in the Spirit'. Although discernment is needed in these circumstances, it is usually better to continue ministering to others and leave the individual to 'rest in the Spirit'. Ministering in a carpeted area is advisable.

It is important that people who have received the healing ministry do not stop taking prescribed medication without first consulting their doctors.

Settings for ministry

As far as possible the environment should be suitable – safe, clean, well-lit, suitably heated and ventilated, with comfortable seating provided and access and facilities available for elderly and disabled people. A quiet, peaceful and reverent atmosphere is conducive to the healing ministry.

It is helpful to distinguish between and adapt to the different kinds of places in which the healing ministry is offered, for example, healing services in church, ministry to the sick in hospital and at home, healing ministry at conferences and healing centres. If ministering to someone in the home setting, care should be taken to avoid informality slipping into, or appearing to become, inappropriate intimacy.

Situations to avoid

These include avoiding, in the context of the healing ministry, interviewing or ministering to persons of the opposite sex, children and adolescents on one's own. It is advisable to avoid having two or more men ministering to a woman alone; whenever possible someone should be involved who is the same gender as the person receiving this ministry.

Clergy and others involved in the healing ministry should take sensible steps to protect themselves from possible physical risk or scandalous accusations when visiting members of the local community, particularly those not already known or those known to have behavioural problems. It is also preferable to avoid late night visits from people not already known, if no one else is around to assist/witness in case of unexpected behaviour.

Where practical, it is advisable for clergy and licensed lay ministers who are single or working alone to ensure that details (name, address, date, etc.) of pastoral visits are known to others, within the boundaries of confidentiality.

Social and cultural contexts

Clergy and lay team members need to be aware of the context in which the healing ministry is being carried out and to be sensitive to the world-view of the parishioner. The social and cultural backgrounds of some people predispose them to beliefs in, for example, superstitions and curses. They may have dabbled in the occult or New Age practices and they may have confused Christian teaching with that of other religions. Social and cultural backgrounds may also influence or mask family tensions. It is important to be aware of the possibility of people's behaviour being affected by substance abuse.

Spiritual dangers

These include:

❖ concentration on self – wanting to be a 'healer' rather than a channel for healing;

❖ residual doubt about the authority of God;

❖ uncritical use of the gift of discernment, and lack of discernment concerning those who claim to have this gift;

❖ enthroning, through overemphasis, the powers of evil rather than Christ;

❖ personality cults: it is advisable to work in pairs and/or teams and change partners when appropriate.

Supervision

Clergy and lay team members should be aware of the need for and benefits of supervision in some related areas of activity, for example the provision of counselling, spiritual direction, deliverance ministry and bereavement counselling.

Support networks

The healing ministry can be stressful and the particular strains it places on those involved in it need to be acknowledged. Those involved have a responsibility to seek adequate support for their own needs and should make sure that they know what facilities are available for them to receive counselling if necessary and that they have adequate rest, quiet days, retreats and spiritual direction.

Teams (see also **Confidentiality** and **Records**)

Sound leadership and good communication are essential for effective teamwork. Team leaders have a responsibility to show reasonableness and consideration towards members and trainees. They have responsibility for ensuring that members have proper training and that relevant gifts within the healing ministry are developed without any sense of competition.

Team members, who should have the respect and trust of their congregation, PCC and parish priest, have joint responsibility for their actions and omissions. Clergy and team leaders should ensure that everyone involved in this ministry is fully aware of and accepts these guidelines. Those who prove to be unsuitable should cease to be involved. The onus should not be on the unsuitable to do the proving; it is the responsibility of the leader to remove such persons from the team if they are not willing to step down voluntarily.

Testimonies (see also **Confidentiality**)

Testimonies can be of considerable value in the context of a healing service. Those who give testimonies, however, should always bear in mind that they will be addressing some who have not received the healing they had hoped for through the Church's healing ministry. Sensitivity, humility and encouragement are more appropriate and helpful than triumphant speeches. It is wise to allow at least a month after experiencing God's healing touch before inviting someone to testify to this.

Thanksgiving

Praise and thanks should be offered to God, in every time of ministry, for the healing received and prayers, too, that the healing given will continue. The Eucharist is the highest liturgical celebration of thanksgiving for healing.

Timing

Reasonable time limits on healing sessions and services should be set. It is important to avoid protracted sessions which overtire those ministering and those receiving; prayer for individuals in a healing service should not become an opportunity for counselling. Knowing when to stop is just as important as knowing when to start. Some people in the congregation may be ill and an hour-long service, for example, may be too long. Provision and permission for them to come and go can be helpful.

Traditions

Respect for the traditions and spiritual experience of other Christians will help to show that different approaches are complementary, rather than mutually exclusive. God works in different ways in different circumstances, responding to infinite varieties of need.

Training, teaching and preaching about the healing ministry

All those involved in the healing ministry should accept the need for preparatory and ongoing training and supervision. Ministers and leaders of healing teams should also accept personal responsibility for keeping up to date with the contemporary healing scene and ensure that they are trained in the wider healing ministry, both initially and for continuous training of themselves and others.

No one should act in isolation; all should be trained as part of being 'under authority'. Personal appraisal should include an assessment of training resources and opportunities to develop awareness and appreciation of other approaches and resources needed. A church congregation involved in this ministry needs to be encouraged to give thought to its own need to be prepared and trained beforehand, and to appraise its progress.

Because there are many misunderstandings about the healing ministry, any suitable opportunities which arise to preach and teach soundly about it should be taken up. The public need help to become more aware of this ministry, to develop their understanding of it, and where and how it can be found locally.

Working with other people involved in caring and healing

The healing ministry is never isolated from the wider setting of the Church and society. Other people are usually involved, including:

❖ professionals involved in medicine and provision of health care, social and community workers;

❖ family and friends, neighbours and work colleagues;

❖ where possible, members of the medical and caring professions in the congregation;

❖ the wider Church structures.

Collaboration and cooperation, based on recognition and respect between ministers and these groups are important factors in helping parishioners towards healing and wholeness.

Appendix 1

House of Bishops' Draft Guidelines for Good Practice in the Healing Ministry

The healing ministry is Jesus' ministry entrusted to us, always to be exercised with reverence, love and compassion. The guiding principle is to recognize the presence of God in those receiving this ministry and honour his presence in them.

1. **Prayer and preparation.** The healing ministry is based on prayer in the name of Jesus Christ; those involved in this ministry should be prayerful, regularly practising Christians who acknowledge his healing love and are willing to pray and listen for guidance in order to minister appropriately to others.

2. **Safety.** All reasonable steps should be taken to ensure the safety of the person receiving this ministry. People have a right to know what is being provided and how they will be ministered to.

3. **Accountability and diocesan regulations.** Everyone involved in the healing ministry needs clear lines of accountability to recognize who holds relevant authority within their parish church. All reasonable steps should be taken by those involved to ensure their awareness of current law as it applies to this ministry, for example data protection; informed consent. Legal liability issues must be considered from an insurance viewpoint. Existing diocesan regulations should also be followed.

4. **Training.** Individuals should receive appropriate training in this ministry and be kept up to date with developments and its ecumenical expression. Healing team leaders must ensure that members have opportunities for training and a common understanding of good practice.

5. **Competence and boundaries.** Persons in this ministry should be aware of their personal limitations and ensure that they are properly prepared and fit to be involved. If fitness is doubtful or compromised or there is a conflict of interests, they should withdraw from ministering to others. Professional boundaries with health care professionals and chaplaincies should be observed.

6. **Personal conduct.** The healing ministry is part of the message of the gospel; the personal conduct of everyone involved should encourage confidence in this ministry and not undermine it. Language, personal hygiene, general appearance, body language and touch used by those ministering should be appropriate, considerate and courteous towards those receiving it. No one should be ministered to against their will.

7. **Confidentiality and public statements.** People's privacy and dignity should be respected and protected. Any limitations to confidentiality should be explained in advance and any disclosure should be restricted to relevant information. It should be conveyed only to appropriate people, normally with the parishioner's consent, and not misused in any way.

8. **Counselling and psychotherapy.** These specific treatments, as distinct from pastoral care and listening, should only be provided by accredited counsellors and therapists who adhere to the codes of ethics and practice of their regulatory organizations and who have professional insurance cover.

9. **Deliverance.** The House of Bishops' guidelines (1975) should be followed and diocesan advisors consulted when necessary.

10. **Partnership.** The healing ministry should be carried out in cooperation, where appropriate, with chaplains and representatives of our ecumenical partners, and those involved in professional and voluntary health care, whilst recognizing that they may be bound by other codes of conduct.

Appendix 2

Sample Pew Leaflet

The sample pew leaflet on the next two pages may be used by churches to inform enquirers about the healing ministry. The pages may be photocopied onto both sides of an A4 sheet and folded to make a four-page booklet.

What are the most common forms of healing ministry?

Public and private prayers of intercession. Christian worship has always included prayers of intercession customarily addressed to the Father through the Son and in the power of the Holy Spirit. Intercessory prayer, in which we pray individually and corporately, for those who are suffering, combines our love with God's love and our will with his will, so as to cooperate with him in fostering his kingdom.

The laying on of hands. Actions can often speak louder than words and touch conveys a message of love and assurance as well as being a link with Christ's apostolic command to heal the sick. Hands are usually placed gently on or side by side of a person's head, or on his or her shoulders and accompanying prayers said quietly and reverently. This form of touch can make a sick person feel less fearful or alone in their suffering.

Anointing. We pray that as we are outwardly anointed with oil, we shall be inwardly anointed with the Holy Spirit. It is customary for a priest to anoint a person with thumb or forefinger, making the sign of the cross, with a small amount of oil on the forehead and sometimes the palms of the hands. Anointing is often accompanied by the laying on of hands and sometimes Holy Communion and reconciliation.

Reconciliation and Absolution. Confession is increasingly seen as an act of reconciliation which begins with God calling us back to himself. The Anglican tradition values the use of a general confession as a communal act in the liturgy and makes provision for private confession to a priest. Private confession may be made in a formal or less formal setting and may include spiritual advice and counsel as well as absolution.

Friendship, forgiveness, listening, acceptance and affirmation can also have a healing grace. So in different ways we are all able to take part in the Church's healing ministry, looking forward in faith to the kind of healing he wills for those for whom we are praying.

The healing ministry is available in the following ways:

❖ **publicly** as part of services;

❖ **at healing services,** including the Eucharist, in institutions such as hospitals, hospices, nursing homes, residential homes for elderly and disabled people, prisons, etc. and at healing centres and related conferences;

❖ **privately** within the home, hospitals and hospices, and discreetly in church side chapels, etc;

❖ **ecumenically** across the denominations, including local services, the hospital and prison chaplaincies;

❖ **in cooperation with the medical and caring professions.**

What can we hope for through this ministry?

We believe that God loves us and wills the very best for us. But we also know that suffering of all kinds and ultimately death are conditions from which we cannot escape. But God is not distant. In Jesus Christ he shared in this life's suffering and death on the cross, and he can draw close to us in times such as these. However, his resurrection in the power of the Holy Spirit gives us hope that we might have a foretaste of his kingdom here and now and that through the Church's ministry we shall receive his love, strength and healing touch. What form that healing will take we cannot tell:

It may be:

❖ help to carry us through a prolonged illness or disability;

❖ a recovery more rapid than expected;

❖ experiencing our fear of death being driven out by God's love;

❖ a healing which is so unexpected that we immediately want to thank God.

The Church of England has recently published a detailed report called *A Time to Heal* (Church House Publishing) which contains a great deal of information and guidance on the healing ministry and has also produced new services for healing and wholeness.

The healing ministry is for everyone; we all need healing in some way. Through the healing ministry, Jesus Christ meets us at our point of need.

THE CHURCH'S HEALING MINISTRY

The Healing Ministry is:

VISIONARY . . . because it beckons us towards the future and a glimpse of the kingdom, and the hope of the whole of creation renewed.

PROPHETIC . . . because it calls us to reconsider our relationships with God, each other and the world and to seek forgiveness and a new start in our lives.

DYNAMIC . . . because Jesus Christ is with us to the end of time: when we pray for his help, he comforts, strengthens and heals us, responding to our deepest needs.

The Church's ministry is a continuation of the ministry of Jesus Christ. We seek to fulfil it in the power of the same Holy Spirit who anointed Jesus at his baptism in the Jordan. Jesus' ministry was totally faithful and obedient to his Father. The gospel of the kingdom of God is the good news of healing which Jesus proclaimed. 'Go and preach the gospel . . . Go and heal the sick' summarizes the commission Christ gave to his Church. So Christians have always been called to have a special concern for those sick in mind, body and spirit. The Church's ministry can be described as one of healing – the healing of ourselves, and of our relationships with God, with one another and with our environment.

Appendix 3

Recommended Reading

Robina Coker, *Alternative Medicine: Helpful or Harmful?*, Monarch Publications, 1995.

Ian Cowie, *Prayers and Ideas for Healing Services*, Wild Goose Publications, 1995.

Martin Dudley and Geoffrey Rowell (eds), *The Oil of Gladness: Anointing in the Christian Tradition*, SPCK, 1993.

Margaret Guenther, *Holy Listening: The Art of Spiritual Direction*, Darton, Longman & Todd, 1992.

John Gunstone, *Prayers for Healing*, Highland Books, 1992.

George Hacker, *The Healing Stream: Catholic Insights into the Ministry of Healing*, Darton, Longman & Todd, 1998.

Gerard Hughes, *God of Compassion*, Hodder & Stoughton, 1998.

Roy Lawrence, *The Practice of Christian Healing*, Triangle, 1998.

Kenneth Leech, *Soul Friend: Spiritual Direction in the Modern World*, Darton, Longman & Todd, 1994.

Anne Long, *Listening*, Darton, Longman & Todd, 1990.

Francis MacNutt, *Healing*, Hodder & Stoughton, 1996.

Morris Maddocks, *The Christian Healing Ministry*, SPCK, 1990.

Michael Mitton and Russ Parker, *Requiem Healing*, Darton, Longman & Todd, 1991.

Russ Parker, *Forgiveness is Healing*, Darton, Longman & Todd, 1993.

Althea Pearson, *Growing Through Loss and Grief*, Marshall Pickering, 1998.

John Penton, *Widening the Eye of the Needle: Access to Church Buildings for People with Disabilities*, Church House Publishing, 1999.

Michael Perry, *Gods Within: A Critical Guide to the New Age*, SPCK, 1992.

Michael Perry, *Deliverance*, SPCK, 1996.

John Richards, *The Question of Healing Services*, Darton, Longman & Todd, 1989.

Barbara Shlemon Ryan, Dennis Linn and Matthew Linn, *To Heal as Jesus Healed*, Resurrection Press, 1997.

Averil Stedeford, *Facing Death*, Heinemann Medical, 1988.

Graham Twelftree, *Christ Triumphant*, Hodder & Stoughton, 1985.

John Wilkinson, *The Bible and Healing: A Medical and Theological Commentary*, Handsel/Eerdmans, 1998.